How to Face Your FAILURES

How to Face Your FAILURES

Dr. Jimmie A. Ellis, III

Copyright © 2009 by Dr. Jimmie A. Ellis, III. All rights reserved.

Printed in the United States of America

Publishing services by Selah Publishing Group, LLC, Tennessee. The views expressed or implied in this work do not necessarily reflect those of Selah Publishing Group.

No part of this publication may be reproduced, stored in a retrieval system or transmitted in any way by any means, electronic, mechanical, photocopy, recording or otherwise, without the prior permission of the author except as provided by USA copyright law.

ISBN: 978-1-58930-233-4
Library of Congress Control Number: 2009901951

I dedicate this book to all those who have tried and failed.

KEEP ON TRYING!!!

Contents

Introduction . . . . *ix*

How to Face Your Failures 11
Reasons for Failure 17
The Results of Failure 23
Remedies for Failure 27

About the Author *31*

Introduction

Does failure defeat you or do you allow failure to make you quit? Have you had high expectations that weren't met? Has your failure caused you to consider giving up your salvation? Quitting is never the answer. Success is built on the back of failure. Every successful person has experienced failure at some point along the way.

Failure is defined as a breakdown in operation/function or not succeeding in doing/becoming. Unfortunately, many people believe that an instance of failure means they themselves are a failure. They become so discouraged that they have mental breakdowns, contemplate suicide, or turn to drugs and alcohol for comfort. We need to remember that failure is an "experience" not a life sentence.

Because we are human, we are not perfect. We will face failure at some point in our lives, but we can thank God that He doesn't close the door on us. He gives us another chance and uses our failures to draw us closer to Him.

Introduction

How to Face Your Failures will teach you how to grow past your failures and continue to be what God wants you to be. Reject the lies Satan uses to convince you that you must be perfect in order to be used by God. Even though you've made mistakes, God CAN and WILL continue to use you. You are His workmanship created in Christ Jesus and He shall perfect those things that concern you. Use the little specks of failure as a platform to rise to greatness!

HOW TO FACE YOUR FAILURES

> **And it came to pass, when David and his men were come to Ziklag on the third day, that the Amalekites had invaded the south, and Ziklag, and smitten Ziklag, and burned it with fire; And had taken the women captives, that were therein: they slew not any, either great or small, but carried them away, and went on their way. So David and his men came to the city, and, behold, it was burned with fire; and their wives, and their sons, and their daughters, were taken captives.**
> 1 SAMUEL 30:1-3

Everyone has experienced failure. The Word of God gives us an example of a man who experienced failure. His name is David. From the scripture we learn that Ziklag was a city the Philistines had given to David. Ziklag, however, was burned and the families who'd lived there had been taken captive. This made David feel as if he had failed. It seemed their mission to overtake the city was unsuccessful.

What is failure? It is a shattering of expectations. Although people aim for success, failure is just as real. It is interwoven within our humanness. We rise to greatness based upon the little specks of failure that we experience.

Even though we are saved and born again, we are still human. In 2 Corinthians 4:7 we read: "But we have this treasure in earthen vessels that the excellency of the power may be of God and not of us." Earthen vessels are described or defined as "clay pots". The term "clay pots" means we are subject to becoming cracked. We often experience failure when we become prideful or believe we are too good to fail. God knows that we are clay pots, but He sees fit to put His treasure within us.

My aim is to help you move beyond your failures to become what God wants you to be. You **CAN** succeed even if you've had a divorce or fallen into sin. You don't have to be perfect to be used by God. I am not perfect, but despite the mistakes I've made, God continues to use me. I had to learn to move beyond my doubts and fears so that I could become what God wants me to be. God is no respecter of persons and if I can accomplish the things that God has commanded of me, so can you.

In Psalms 103:13-14 we read:

> **Like as a father pitieth his children, so the LORD pitieth them that fear him. For he knoweth our frame; he remembereth that we are dust.**

God still wants to use us and He continues to work on us as we do His will. God won't stop blessing because there is a recession. Prosperity is still in the land. People continue to graduate and earn degrees while they are doing God's will.

Don't become discourage when people speak negatively about you because:

> **For their heart was not right with him, neither were they stedfast in his covenant. But he, being full of compassion, forgave their iniquity, and destroyed them not: yea, many a time turned he his anger away, and did not stir up all his wrath. For he remembered that they were but flesh; a wind that passeth away, and cometh not again.**
> **PSALM 78:37-39**

Failure is sprinkled in with our success. All great people of God have faced failure:

1. Peter
2. Joseph
3. Job

There are modern-day people who encountered failure before they achieved success:

1. Abraham Lincoln had a difficult childhood. He failed in business and was defeated for political office. He tried and failed a second time in business. One year later he was elected to legislature, but his fiancé died one year later. He campaigned to be Speaker of the House, but was defeated. He was defeated yet again when he tried to be an Elector in the Senate. Two years later, he married Mary, but it was not a happy marriage. He had four sons, but only one lived to be 18 years old. At first he was defeated for Congress, but was elected three years later. He ran for re-election twice again and was defeated both times. When he ran for Vice President of the United States, he was defeated. Once gain he decided to run for a seat in the Senate and again was defeated. Despite all these defeats he had the courage to campaign for the presidency. He won!!! Abraham Lincoln proved to be one of the greatest Presidents we have ever known. I want you to see that successful people have the fingerprints of failure in their lives.

WALT DISNEY
- Fired by a newspaper editor for a lack of ideas
- Went bankrupt several times
- Finally built Disney Land

Thomas Edison
- Told by a teacher he was too stupid to learn anything
- His parents concurred with his teachers

Albert Einstein
- Didn't speak until he was 4 years old
- Was unable to read until he was 7 year old
- Told by a teacher he was mentally slow, unsociable and would drift forever in his foolish dreams
- Was suspended from one school and denied admittance to a Poly-Technical School.

Henry Ford
- Was bankrupt five times before he designed the Ford car

Winston Churchill
- Failed the 6th grade
- Experienced a lifetime of setbacks and other failures
- Became Prime Minister of England when he was 62 years old

Beethoven

- Handled the violin awkwardly, but decided to play his own compositions rather than improve his technique.
- His teacher called him hopeless as a composer.

Although these people experienced failure, they eventually found success. Jesus is our High Priest because he is touched with our failures.

REASONS FOR FAILURE

Sometimes we are at fault when we fail. Other times, we fail because things are out of our control. We are at fault for our failures when we:

1. Make Bad Choices

This happens when major decisions are made quickly without seeking God's counsel or that of wise advisors. As a result, we fail. Joshua made this mistake.

> **And when the inhabitants of Gibeon heard what Joshua had done unto Jericho and to Ai, they did work willingly, and went and made as if they had been ambassadors, and took old sacks upon their asses, and wine bottles, old, and rent, and bound up; And old shoes and clouted upon their feet, and old garments upon them; and all the bread of their provision was dry and mouldy. And they went to Joshua unto the camp**

> **at Gilgal, and said unto him, and to the men of Israel, We be come from a far country: now therefore make ye a league with us. And the men took of their victuals, and asked not counsel at the mouth of the LORD.**
> JOSHUA 9:3-6 & 14

Joshua made a bad decision because he did not ask the Lord. His bad choices caused him to fail.

2. WE ARE HEADED IN THE WRONG DIRECTION

We experience failure when we rebel against God and decided to do what **WE** want to do. We fail to pray and don't take the necessary time to make a wise decision. We don't want to wait. We want what we want **WHEN** we want it. David is a perfect example. He felt that he had to have Bethsheeba and it caused him to fail. (2 Samuel 12)

We are **NOT** at fault for our failures when:

1. WE ARE CONNECTED TO THE WRONG PEOPLE

Sometimes we fail because we are involved with the wrong people. These people are in our lives either by skill or spirit. People can cause you to fail if they are not skillful enough or don't have the right spirit. If you want to begin a business or start a church, you must surround yourself with the right types of people. They don't have to be **PERFECT**, but they must have the right spirit and possess the necessary skills.

> **But the children of Israel committed a trespass in the accused thing: for Achan, the son of Carmi, the son of Zabdi, the son of Zerah, of the tribe of Judah, took of the accursed thing: and the anger of the LORD was kindled against the children of Israel. And the LORD said unto Joshua, Get thee up; wherefore liest thou thus upon thy face? Israel hath sinned, and they have also transgressed my covenant which I commanded them: for they have even taken of the accursed thing, and have also stolen, and dissembled also, and they have put it even among their own stuff.**
> JOSHUA 7:1, 10-11

Achan had stolen a Babylonian garment from Jericho and it caused the entire nation to fail. You can be connected to someone who causes you to fail. Even though they may have the necessary skill to work with you, they may not have the right spirit.

How can you determine if someone has your spirit? By their wisdom. We make the mistake of thinking that knowledge and wisdom are one and the same. They are not. When you go to church, you gain knowledge, but you will not gain wisdom until you work the principles of the Bible. It does no good for a child to know the ABCs if he doesn't understand how to use them to form sentences. That child will have KNOWLEDGE, but not WISDOM.

It serves no purpose to have someone with you who just repeats what you say without having wisdom. Even if that person does have wisdom, if he doesn't have the right spirit, he will still cause you to fail. Sometimes it is better to be alone than to be hooked up with the wrong person.

> **Therefore the children of Israel could not stand before their enemies, but turned their backs before their enemies, because they were accursed: neither will I be with you any more, except ye destroy the accursed from among you.**
> **JOSHUA 7:12**

They were cursed because they had a relationship with Achan.

2. We Are In The Wrong Season

In Ecclesiastes 3:1-8, we learn that there is a season for everything in life:

> **To every thing there is a season, and a time to every purpose under the heaven: A time to be born, and a time to die; a time to plant, and a time to pluck up that which is planted; A time to kill, and a time to heal; a time to break down, and a time to build up; A time to weep, and a time to laugh; a time to mourn, and a time to dance; A time to cast away stones, and a time to gather stones together; a time to embrace, and a time to refrain from embracing; A time to get, and a time to lose; a time to keep, and a time to cast away; A time to rend, and a time to sew; a time to keep silence, and a time to speak; A time to love, and a time to hate; a time of war, and a time of peace.**

There is a season for every event in our lives. There is a time for us to experience success and a time for us to experience failure. You may currently be in a season of failure, but there is a season of success coming. We sometimes blame ourselves for our failures, but we may not be at fault. We may simply not be in our season of success.

3. THE ENEMY

> **Another parable put he forth unto them, saying, The kingdom of heaven is likened unto a man which sowed good seed in his field: But while men slept, his enemy came and sowed tares among the wheat, and went his way.**
> **MATTHEW 13:24-25**

Sometimes the devil will sneak in and sow failure in our lives. We cannot always prevent failure, but we can stop failure from controlling us.

THE RESULTS OF FAILURE

1. DISTRESS OF SOUL

Then David and the people that were with him lifted up their voice and wept, until they had no more power to weep. And David was greatly distressed; for the people spake of stoning him, because the soul of all the people was grieved, every man for his sons and for his daughters: but David encouraged himself in the LORD his God.

David is feeling distressed because he was being blamed for getting everyone into a mess. Everyone was upset. Even David, the anointed one, was stressed. Contrary to the teachings of our culture, it does NOT make a man less manly to show emotions. If we attempt to contain our stress, it will make itself evident in our behavior. We may begin to smoke, drink alcohol or engage in other sinful/harmful behaviors. It is healthier to confront our stress head on and deal with it.

2. Dismissal Of Purpose

Peter almost experienced the loss of his purpose. When he failed, he was so discouraged that he wanted to give up and go back to fishing. When we fail, we can become so depressed that we begin to feel like a hypocrite. We decide we won't pick up a Bible ever again.

> **After these things Jesus shewed himself again to the disciples at the sea of Tiberias; and on this wise shewed he himself. There were together Simon Peter, and Thomas called Didymus, and Nathanael of Cana in Galilee, and the sons of Zebedee, and two other of his disciples. Simon Peter saith unto them, I go a fishing. They say unto him, We also go with thee. They went forth, and entered into a ship immediately; and that night they caught nothing. So when they had dined, Jesus saith to Simon Peter, Simon, son of Jonas, lovest thou me more than these?**
> JOHN 21:1-3 & 15A

Let us understand that God is not going to give up on us because we fail. Jesus didn't abandon Peter, but gave him an opportunity to restore their relationship.

3. WE ARE DRIVEN TO GOD

Our failures will sometimes drive us to God. When David failed, he turned to the Lord. He cried out to God and encouraged himself in the Lord. Now I don't believe that David was trying to recall scripture. Scripture just returned to his memory. When we are experiencing difficulties, God, through the Holy Spirit, will minister to us.

When we are depressed, the Word that we have hidden in our hearts will come forth to minister to us. The Lord Himself will encourage us to get up, brush off the dust, get dressed and head off to church. Through His Word, God will remind us that we are **NOT** alone. He wants us to remember that greater is He who is within us than he who is in the world. God starts talking to us when we are at the low points. When our hearts/minds are telling us to quit, God will tell us to keep going. He will tell us to continue singing on the choir, ushering/greeting, preparing the meals or doing whatever He has called us to do.

Don't let the devil steal what God has planted within you!

4. Lean On Your Spiritual Resources

When you are feeling out of control, return to your spiritual resources. When you don't know what do to and have run out of ideas, return to your spiritual resources. Get on your knees and pray in the spirit until you strike oil. Wisdom is not on the surface, it is a treasure to be sought. Wisdom is like gold buried in the ground and we must dig down deep if we want to find it.

REMEDIES FOR FAILURE

1. Face The Fact That You Have Failed

It is sometimes difficult to admit that we have failed. Admitting failure is an act of humility that makes us feel low and weak. We try hard to avoid admitting defeat because society makes us think we have to be perfect at at everything. The fact is that we are **NOT** perfect at anything and the ability to face this truth moves us closer to success. Facing our weaknesses brings us closer to Jesus Christ. He is able to feel our pain and disappointments and wants us to come to Him so that He can intervene and redirect us.

2. Forgive Yourself

It is difficult for us to forgive ourselves when we've failed. The guilt and shame of not achieving our desired goals are quite painful. This is when we have to rely on the Lord to strengthen our hearts so we can move on. If we don't forgive ourselves, we hamper our own success. It is important that we let go of everything and everyone that caused our failure. To do this will take the power of God.

Without God's help and guidance, unforgiveness will overtake our hearts. We may be able to move on, but bitterness and unforgiveness will block the path to success.

3. Realize That You Are NOT Finished

You may have failed, but you are not a failure. Failure can cause us to think that we are finished and that there is no meaning or purpose to our lives. That is a lie from Satan! God has a purpose and plan for all of His children. We must remember that God does not think of us as failures because He is the one who created us. He knew from the beginning that we would miss the mark, make mistakes and fall short. Failure does NOT mean that our lives are over. We simply must continue to push forward and have faith to believe that God will see us through.

4. Focus On The Lessons You Have Learned

There are lessons to be learned from failure. When we fail we usually begin to focus on ourselves and others. When we do this, we find:

A. Redirection
B. Renewal
C. Replacement

5. Fight The Feelings Of Shame And Embarrassment

It is very important that we not allow ourselves to be overwhelmed with feelings of shame or embarrassment. If we do, the devil will convince us that the world is coming to an end.

6. Forget The Failure And Keep On Moving

Don't wallow in your failure. Many who don't know the Lord have failed but went on to find success and redemption. Mickey Rourke was written off when he failed, but he stayed in the game and won a Golden Globe for his portrayal of a wrestler. Robert Downey, Jr. was cast aside for his failures, but he rebounded and found success again. If the unsaved can recover from failure, how much more can those who know the Lord. We have the Almighty God on our side and He will give us every opportunity to bounce back when we fail. We don't fail because we fall, we fail when we refuse to get up and start over again!!!

Don't let the devil steal your destiny!!!! Get up, dust yourself off and start all over again. God is routing for you!!!!

About the Author

In 1985, Dr. Ellis founded Arnaz Ministries School of the Word Bible Institute. As Founder and President, Dr. Ellis designed a curriculum to train individuals who've been called to a five-fold ministry, the ministry of counseling, and those who desire an in-depth study of the Word of God for spiritual fulfillment. Today, the two-year program offers a variety of selective and innovative courses conducive to developing church leaders of all facets.

In 1999, Dr. Ellis founded The Conquerors Community Development Corporation (CCDC), a mission designed to elevate the quality of life for the Southwest Philadelphia community through economic development, child development, technological awareness, spiritual/cultural programs and health initiatives. Dr. Ellis' vision is to further institute employment services, daycare services,

About the Author

housing and community revitalization programs, health related projects and life skills to empower the community.

In March 2004, Dr. Ellis received his honorary Doctorate of Divinity Degree from Saint Thomas Christian College in Jacksonville, Florida. Dr. Ellis' contributions have been applauded throughout the city by the media, governing officials and with numerous awards.

To order additional copies of

How to Face Your
Failures

have your credit card ready and call
1 800-917-BOOK (2665)

or e-mail
orders@selahbooks.com

or order online at
www.selahbooks.com

Printed in the United States
141912LV00001B/4/P